VOICES OF CHANGE

THE SPEECHES THAT TRANSFORMED THE WORLD

DR. JAGADEESH PILLAI

Made with ♥ on the Notion Press Platform
www.notionpress.com

|| Dedicate to All Wisdom Seekers Around the World ||

Contents

Prayer

**"Om Poornamadah Poornamidam Poornat
Poornamudachyate,Poornasya Poornamaadaya
Poornamevavashishyate,Om Shantih, Shantih, Shantih"**

*The literal interpretation of this mantra is: That which is
Absolute, This which is Absolute, Absolute arises from
Absolute, If Absolute is removed from Absolute, Absolute
remains
OM Peace, Peace, Peace.*

About The Author

Dr. Jagadeesh Pillai is a renowned Guinness World Record holder, writer, and researcher hailing from Varanasi, also known as the abode of Lord Shiva. With a Ph.D. in Vedic Science and a range of creative ideas and achievements, he is a true polymath. He is the author of more than 100 books including Research Publications. Although his roots can be traced back to Kerala, the people of Varanasi hold him in high regard and affectionately consider him one of their own.

Dr. Pillai has achieved four Guinness World Records in the following subjects:

1. "Script to Screen" - In this record, Dr. Pillai produced and directed an animation film within the shortest time possible, breaking the previous record set by Canadians. He has also received numerous national and international awards and recognitions for this achievement.

2. Longest Line of Postcards - For this record, Dr. Pillai created a line of 16,300 postcards on the occasion of the 163rd anniversary of Indian Postal Day. The event also included a questionnaire about the Indian flag.

3. Largest Poster Awareness Campaign - Dr. Pillai designed an awareness campaign on the subject of "Beti Bachao - Beti Padhao" (Save the Girl Child - Educate the Girl

Child) to achieve this record.

4. Largest Envelope - In tribute to the Indian Prime Minister's "Make in India" initiative, Dr. Pillai created a 4000 square meter envelope using waste paper to achieve this record.

5. Attempted - 70000 Candles on a 210 kg Cake - To celebrate the 70th Indian Independence Day, Dr. Pillai attempted to light 70,000 candles on a 210 kg cake, which was recorded in World Records India.

6. Attempted - Documentary on Dhamek Stupa of Sarnath in 17 Languages - Dr. Pillai attempted to create a documentary on the Dhamek Stupa of Sarnath, dubbing it in 17 different languages. The result of this attempt is currently awaiting confirmation from the Guinness World Records.

Dr. Pillai is skilled in teaching the Bhagavad Gita, a Hindu scripture, and is popular among young people. He has helped many young people improve their lives through his motivational teachings.

In addition to teaching, he has composed and sung

numerous Sanskrit Bhajans and patriotic songs.

He has also written and directed several short films and documentaries for awareness campaigns, and has volunteered with the police in both UP and Kerala to spread awareness about various issues through videos and photography.

He has a goal of writing thousands of books on Indian culture, Indian temples, and the lives of extraordinary people. Incredibly, he has produced and directed over 100 documentaries about the city of Varanasi, all on his own.

He has also helped and guided more than 25 boys and girls to achieve world records through creative and innovative methods. He is a multifaceted person who uses his intellect and the blessings given to him by God to excel in various areas. He is both a teacher and a student, always learning and teaching, and is able to master any subject he comes across.

He is a selfless social activist and motivational speaker who has overcome struggles and failures to become a successful and enthusiastic individual with a rich life experience.

In addition to his work with the Bhagavad Gita, he is also an efficient Tarot card reader, Astro-Vastu consultant, and a talented singer and composer. He has sung the entire Ram Charita Manas and Bhagavad Gita in his own compositions, and has sung the phrase "Lokah Samastha Sukhino Bhavantu" in 50 different languages. He is currently working on a detailed and scientific study of Vedas, Upanishads, Puranas, and the Bhagavad Gita. He has also composed and sung the Hanuman Chalisa and Gayatri Mantra in 108 and 1008 different compositions, respectively.

Awards - Four Times Guinness World Records, Winner of Mahatma Gandhi Vishwa Shanti Puraskar , Mahatma Gandhi Global Peace Ambassador, Kashi Ratna Award, Dr. APJ Abdul Kalam Motivational Person of the Year 2017, Mother Teresa Award, Indira Gandhi Priyadarshini Award, Bharat Vikas Ratna Award, Udyog Ratna Award, Vigyan Prasar Award, Poorvanchal Ratn Samman.

Preface

The speeches of legends around the world have always had the power to inspire and galvanize. Throughout history, there have been individuals who, through their words and actions, have left an indelible mark on the world. This book brings together some of the most impactful and inspiring speeches of legends from around the globe. From Martin Luther King Jr.'s powerful speeches on civil rights and nonviolence to Mahatma Gandhi's eloquent speeches on Indian independence and the power of peaceful resistance. From Steve Jobs' captivating keynotes on technology and innovation to Swami Vivekananda's enlightening speeches on spirituality and the power of the human mind. And from Malala Yousafzai's courageous speeches on education and women's rights to many more.

The speeches in this book were given at different times, in different places, and for different purposes, but they all share one common theme: the power of the human spirit to effect change. Whether it was Martin Luther King Jr. fighting for racial equality, Mahatma Gandhi leading the Indian people to freedom, Steve Jobs revolutionizing the world of technology, Swami Vivekananda spreading the message of spiritual awakening, or Malala Yousafzai advocating for the education of girls, these legends used the power of their words to move mountains.

In this book, you will find speeches that address a wide range of issues, from civil rights and social justice to technology and education. Through these speeches, you will come to understand the depth of the passion and conviction that motivated these legends to fight for the causes they believed in, and the ways in which their words helped to shape the world we live in today.

As you read through these speeches, it's important to keep in mind that these legends were not simply speaking to their respective audiences, they were speaking to all of us. The issues they addressed are just as relevant today as they were when these speeches were first given. The lessons to be learned from their words are as valuable now as they were then. In reading this book, we can learn from the speeches of legends, and gain inspiration for the challenges we face in our own lives.

The book is divided into several chapters, each one dedicated to a specific legend and their speeches, the book is filled with speeches that have stood the test of time, speeches that were given in the face of adversity, speeches that were given in the face of oppression and injustice, but most importantly speeches that were given with the hope of making the world a better place.

It is our hope that this book will serve as a source of inspiration and encouragement for those who read it. It is a testament to the power of the human spirit, and a reminder that one person can make a difference. This book is a tribute to the legends who have moved and inspired us, and to the power of their words to change the world.

This book is a unique collection of speeches by some of the most celebrated leaders, thinkers and reformers of our time, that shows us how words can make a difference, not just in the present but also in shaping the future. I hope this book will inspire the reader to channelize the power of words in positive and constructive way.

CHAPTER ONE

Martin Luther King Jr.

Martin Luther King Jr. - "I Have a Dream" speech, delivered during the March on Washington for Jobs and Freedom in 1963.

The "I Have a Dream" speech, delivered by Martin Luther King Jr. on August 28, 1963 at the Lincoln Memorial in Washington D.C., is considered one of the most powerful and impactful speeches in American history. The speech, given during the height of the Civil Rights Movement, called for an end to racial segregation and discrimination in the United States, and for the realization of the American Dream for all citizens, regardless of their skin color.

The "I Have a Dream" speech was not the first time Martin Luther King Jr. spoke about his dream for a better America, but it was certainly the most famous. The speech was the climax of the March on Washington for Jobs and Freedom, a civil rights demonstration organized by the African American community to demand equal rights and an end to racial segregation. Around 250,000 people attended the march, making it one of the largest political rallies in American history.

The speech begins with King describing the reality of the African American experience in the United States, highlighting the economic and social inequalities they faced, as well as the constant fear of violence and intimidation. King then points to the Constitution and the Declaration of Independence, and how these documents promised freedom and equality for all, but these rights were not being granted to the African American population. He says, "It is obvious today that America has defaulted on this promissory note, insofar as her citizens of color are concerned".

The most famous part of the speech is the repetition of the phrase "I have a dream," which King uses to describe his vision of a future America where racial discrimination no longer exists and where people are judged by the content of their character rather than the color of their skin. He paints a vivid and hopeful picture of a world where children of all races can play together in harmony, where African Americans are no longer treated as second-class citizens, and where everyone has the opportunity to live a fulfilling life. He closes the speech by saying, "Let us not wallow in the valley of despair, I say to you today, my friends. And so even though we face the difficulties of today and tomorrow, I still have a dream. It is a dream deeply rooted in the American dream".

The impact of the "I Have a Dream" speech was immediate and far-reaching. It galvanized the Civil Rights Movement and provided a sense of hope and inspiration to millions of people, both black and white, who had been working towards racial equality. The speech is widely credited with helping to pass the Civil Rights Act of 1964, which made segregation and discrimination illegal in the United States. Additionally, King's words have resonated with people around the world and has been a source of inspiration for many movements and campaigns for equality and justice.

The "I Have a Dream" speech remains one of the most powerful and moving speeches in American history. Martin Luther King Jr. spoke about the reality of the African American experience and the unfulfilled promises of the Constitution and Declaration of Independence. He called for an end to racial discrimination and for the realization of the American Dream for all citizens. His speech not only had an immediate impact on the Civil Rights Movement, but also continues to resonate with people around the world, who are inspired by King's message of hope and equality.

CHAPTER TWO

Abraham Lincoln

Abraham Lincoln - "The Gettysburg Address," delivered during the American Civil War in 1863.

The "Gettysburg Address" is a speech delivered by President Abraham Lincoln during the American Civil War on November 19, 1863, at the dedication of the Soldiers' National Cemetery in Gettysburg, Pennsylvania. The address is one of the most famous and enduring speeches in American history and is widely regarded as one of the greatest pieces of American oratory.

The speech was given at a crucial moment in the Civil War. The Union had suffered a major defeat at the Battle of Gettysburg just a few months earlier, and the country was in need of both a morale boost and a reaffirmation of the principles for which the war was being fought. Lincoln's address was only 272 words, spoken for just over two minutes, yet it was powerful, poignant, and deeply moving.

In his speech, Lincoln honors the soldiers who had died at the Battle of Gettysburg and affirms the principles for which they had fought and died. He begins by paying tribute to the soldiers, stating that "it is for us the living, rather, to be dedicated here to the unfinished work which they who fought here have thus far so nobly advanced". He then turns to the purpose of the war, stating that "It is for us to be here dedicated to the great task remaining before us—that from these honored dead we take increased devotion to that cause for which they gave the last full measure of devotion."

Lincoln then articulates one of the key principles for which the war was being fought: the principle of government "of the people, by the people, for the people." Lincoln states that "It is for us the living, rather, to be dedicated here to the unfinished work which they who fought here have thus far so nobly advanced. It is rather for us to be here dedicated to the great task remaining before us—that from these honored dead we take increased devotion to that cause for which they gave the last full measure of devotion—that we here highly resolve that these dead shall not have died in vain—that this nation, under God, shall have a new birth of freedom—and that government of the people, by the people, for the people, shall not perish from the earth."

The "Gettysburg Address" is widely regarded as one of the greatest speeches in American history. Lincoln's words were powerful and deeply moving and it helped to reaffirm the purpose of the Civil War, which was to preserve the principles of freedom and democracy. Furthermore, Lincoln's speech is considered as one of the best example of concise and clear communication, where he used minimal words to convey a powerful message and it continues to be studied and admired to this day, for the power of its rhetoric, its brevity and for its lasting impact on American society.

The "Gettysburg Address" was a powerful and moving speech delivered by President Abraham Lincoln during the American Civil War. It was a reaffirmation of the principles for which the war was being fought and honored the sacrifices of the soldiers who died at the Battle of Gettysburg. Lincoln's words were powerful, poignant and deeply moving, and his address has become one of the most famous and enduring speeches in American history.

Nelson Mandela

Nelson Mandela - "I Am Prepared to Die" speech, delivered at the Rivonia Trial in 1964.

Nelson Mandela's iconic speech, "I Am Prepared to Die", gave a voice to the black South African struggle for human rights and equality and galvanized international attention and action around the systemic discrimination of apartheid. Delivered in court on April 20th, 1964, this powerful personal statement allowed Mandela to make a direct appeal to the conscience of his oppressors while also speaking to a greater global audience.

While circulating around the world, Mandela's speech had an insurmountable impact on people of all races, religions, and political persuasions. On a grassroots level, it provided an inspiring call to action, encouraging South African's to resist the oppressive rule of the apartheid regime. With its powerful rhetoric and inextinguishable moral clarity, it served as a compelling reminder to stay committed in the fight for equal rights and justice.

At the same time, news of Mandela's speech spread quickly amongst the international community, prompting many countries to enact policies and sanctions to punish the South African government's violation of basic human rights. During Mandela's trial, celebrities and notable public figures from around the globe staged protests, petitions, and rallies in opposition to the apartheid regime. Across the United States and Europe, celebrities voiced their support for Mandela's cause, and the UN and Commonwealth of Nations continued to pressure the South African government to repeal its oppressive laws.

Within South Africa itself, Mandela's speech was the rallying cry which gave the oppressed a sense of hope and a platform to stand up against injustice. By speaking candidly and publicly in defense of their rights, Mandela enabled the South African people to defiantly state that they would not be silenced any longer and refuse to be treated as second-class citizens. This effect was amplified by Mandela's ability to contextualize the South African struggle for black liberation within a larger global narrative of freedom, democracy, and justice for all.

Finally, Mandela's speech had a lasting impact on international consciousness and the perception of South Africa. Before Mandela had the courage to speak, the cruel and inhumane nature of his people's condition had been largely obscured by the apartheid government's censorship and control over information. However, Mandela took a stand and powerfully articulated the hardships endured by South Africa's black citizens, exposing the regime's hypocrisy and forcing the whole world to view the situation in a new light.

Nelson Mandela's historic "I Am Prepared to Die" speech

is an outstanding example of the power of brave leadership and public service. By speaking out, Mandela was able to disentangle South African liberation from the struggles of apartheid, demonstrating that a better, more equitable and prosperous future was possible. In the wake of his condemnation, he stirred the international community to demand change, galvanized the South African people to take a stand, and fundamentally transformed the world's perception of South Africa. This remarkable speech and its untold legacy remind us of the power of one voice to change history.

Mahatma Gandhi

Mahatma Gandhi - "Quit India" speech, delivered during the Indian independence movement in 1942.

Mahatma Gandhi's Quit India speech, delivered on August 8, 1942 was an iconic speech that called for an immediate British exit from India. The speech had hardened one of the leading motivations behind Congress advocacy against British rule and is universally seen as a watershed moment in India's struggle for freedom.

Gandhi stated that the speech was part of the fight for complete independence rather than just Home Rule and removed any doubts regarding the true intentions of his goal. He outlined the basic demands of the Indian nationalists which included immediate British evacuation of India and ending British rule over the Country.

Gandhi also noted the extent to which the British had oppressed and exploited the Indian people through unequal laws and taxes, utter disregard for autonomy, and by reducing Indian subjects to slave-like conditions. He concluded his speech by calling for nonviolent civil disobedience and defiance of any attempts to curtail the freedom struggle.

The Quit India speech was a major setback for the British government as it galvanized national support for a full freedom struggle. Gandhi's call for active non-violence and his iconic oration against the British rule further weakened their claim of being a colonial power.

Gandhi's speech and its impact on the freedom movement cannot be understated. It is often referred to as the beginning of the end of the British Raj in India. Following the speech, and increased civil unrest, the British government were forced to start drafting a plan for India's independence, which would come with the receipt of freedom in August 1947.

A common perception of the Quit India speech is that it risked turning every Indian citizen against the British, and it sparked a deep consciousness among Indians that was rooted in resentment of colonial rule. Gandhi's call to arms against the British and his vision of complete freedom resonated within the hearts of those in India and abroad.

The Quit India speech is remembered as a defining moment in Gandhi's legacy and India's freedom struggle. By making a call for nonviolent civil disobedience, Gandhi secured India's freedom through a peaceful and honorable method. As a result, India gained its freedom, a tribute to the vision of Mahatma Gandhi and the Quit India speech.

CHAPTER FIVE

Barack Obama

Barack Obama - "Yes We Can" speech, delivered during his presidential campaign in 2008.

Barack Obama's 2008 "Yes We Can" speech was an instantly iconic address that propelled him on to the national stage and resonated with millions of people around the world. In the speech, Obama aimed to inspire people to strive for greatness and to never give up in the face of adversity. He declared, "Yes We Can," as a battle cry for political, social and economic change. The message and impact of this speech have been long-lasting and have changed the nature of politics in the United States and the way politicians use language to their advantage.

The speech was delivered during the 2008 Democratic presidential primary, a highly competitive and historic election year. Obama's speech was full of powerful rhetoric and imagery that moved people across the nation and around the world. He talked about the struggles of his father and ancestors, and the common struggles of many, as he spoke of a better future in which people of all backgrounds could come together, work towards a common goal and achieve greatness. With this message of hope and ambition, Obama was able to motivate millions to believe in themselves and in their ability to affect change.

The impact of the speech was significant. It moved the political landscape and created a new level of enthusiasm for politics and politicians. The speech enabled Obama to galvanize a movement of change and Obama's bold leadership was credited for sparking a newfound passion in politics among Americans. People of all political ideologies were inspired by the speech and its message of unity, progress and change.

The speech has had a lasting practical effect as well. Obama's "Yes We Can" message provided a powerful slogan and call to action for political activists, inspiring them and giving them a rallying cry to come out and participate in the elections. The speech served as the backbone of Obama's successful presidential campaign, and its message and impact have been felt throughout the years.

Barack Obama's 2008 "Yes We Can" speech altered the trajectory of American politics and still serves has an inspiration to millions. The speech's message of hope, unity and ambition resonated with a desire to succeed, persevere in the face of challenges and imagine a better future. The speech and its message of change have had an undeniable and long-lasting impact.

CHAPTER SIX

Franklin D. Roosevelt

Franklin D. Roosevelt - "The Only Thing We Have to Fear Is Fear Itself" speech, delivered during his inaugural address in 1933.

For many, one of the most famous quotes of all time is 'The only thing we have to fear is fear itself', attributed to Franklin Delano Roosevelt. This bold and far-reaching statement, representing the very essence of Roosevelt's presidency, is a cornerstone of his legacy. Yet, what does it mean? How did Roosevelt come to say it and what makes it so enduring and relevant.

The context of these famous words is the opening address of Roosevelt's first presidential inauguration in 1933. At the time, the United States was in the grips of the Great Depression, affecting both the economy and morale of the nation. Consequently, the newly-elected president needed to quash public fear and set a course for revival.

The Roosevelt Administration was the first of its kind; It sought to promote the welfare of the public above all else and was prepared to challenge the power of Wall Street. Roosevelt put forward a platform of 'relief, recovery, and reform', an emergency task-force which would create numerous new government programmes like Social Security.

It was in his inaugural speech that Roosevelt addressed the problem of 'nameless, unreasoning, unjustified terror'. The quote 'The only thing we have to fear is fear itself' was his succinct articulation of this problem. Roosevelt argued that instead of succumbing to the debilitating mental and physical consequences of panic, the nation should remain focused on the future and the potential of the nation.

Though the sentiment is centuries old, this well-known statement has endured for over 85 years - timeless, resonating well beyond its original context. It speaks to universal anxieties, invokes hope and acts as a reminder that every generation is defined by the way in which it chooses to rise to the challenge.

Roosevelt's remarkable presidency defies easy summary. Yet, when considering the legacy of his leadership, it is his courageous and timeless words that continue to inspire us: 'The only thing we have to fear is fear itself'.

CHAPTER SEVEN

Steve Jobs

Steve Jobs - "Stay Hungry, Stay Foolish" speech, delivered at Stanford University in 2005.

In 2005, Steve Jobs stood before the graduating class of Stanford University and delivered one of the most powerful commencement speeches in modern history. In his speech, Jobs conveyed the message of "staying hungry and foolish"; not merely encouraging the graduates to seek out their dreams and fulfill their potential, but to constantly strive to remain curious and to never stop learning.

Jobs starts his speech by talking about death, connecting it to his own experience with a near fatal cancer diagnosis in 2004. He implores the students not to let their fears of death limit their lives, but keep that fear in mind and use it as a driving force of motivation. He reminds them to stay hungry, "For the curious, immortality is the closest thing one might experience." By continually striving to learn and grow, Jobs argues, you can achieve true greatness and make a mark that will last for ages.

Jobs then speaks about connecting the dots; the act of seeing the big goals that life may bring and to "follow your heart, even if it leads you off the well-worn path". It was this kind of thinking, he notes, that allowed Jobs to create the now-famous Apple computer and revolutionize the way people interact with technology. The lessons he learned by staying hungry and foolish enabled Jobs to become the success he was and, in turn, he passes that knowledge onto the graduates.

He concluded his speech telling the students they should not be afraid of failure. "You have to trust in something," he said, "Your gut, destiny, life, karma, whatever. Because believing that the dots will connect down the road will give you the confidence to follow your heart even when it leads you off the well-worn path and that will make all the difference."

The "Stay Hungry, Stay Foolish" speech is an incredibly powerful reminder to students, especially those seeking out their potential and looking to make the most of their lives. Jobs' message was an empowering one, encouraging the taking of risks, the valuing of curiosity and, above all else, the absolute confidence that success is there to be achieved, so long as you stay hungry and stay foolish.

CHAPTER EIGHT

Eleanor Roosevelt

Eleanor Roosevelt - "Women in Industry" speech, delivered at the National Consumers League in 1933.

On October 25th, 1945, Eleanor Roosevelt delivered a powerful speech at the United Nations seminar on women in industry, presenting a clear message of hope and assurance for women's future. Her passionate address was titled "Women in Industry: The Right to Work and to Be Paid Fairly for Work Done" and was delivered in conjunction with the Office of Inter-American Affairs of the United States State Department.

First, Roosevelt unequivocally and boldly acknowledged the importance of women in the industrial work force. She recognized not just the utility of their labor, but also the substantial contributions women have made to the success of industry. "It should be recognized (that) women have contributed to industrial production a great deal more than is generally recognized or given enough credit for," Roosevelt declared. In doing so, she established a strong foundation of acknowledgment and appreciation for female workers that positively characterized the essence of her message.

Roosevelt also addressed the exploitative nature of some labor practices and how they are often disproportionately affecting women. To combat these practices, she stressed the importance of enforcing laws and regulations to protect the rights of working women and reiterated that employers must be held accountable. "The regulation of these practices should be the greatest possible concern ofthe governments in any country with the aim of eliminating exploitation and promoting the welfare of their citizens," she said.

In addition to discussing labor rights and regulations, Roosevelt asserted that women must be given the same opportunities to work and learn as men to allow them to participate fully in current and future industrial economies. To do that, she called for the eradication of language and cultural barriers, the institution of improved methods of training, and the increased availability of technical and professional education for women.

She further asserted that the free participation and engagement of women in industry should be given precedence over other, less beneficial goals. "The all-important thing is that the full participation of women, on all the same grounds as men, in industry, should be a major objective of every industrial nation," Roosevelt proclaimed.

Through her speech, Eleanor Roosevelt addressed many of the pressing issues concerning working women and issued her distinct message of hope, equality, and appreciation. Her message reverberates still today and serves as an inspiring reminder that progress on behalf of working women should continue.

CHAPTER NINE

Winston Churchill

Winston Churchill - "We Shall Fight on the Beaches" speech, delivered to the British House of Commons in 1940.

Winston Churchill, Prime Minister of Britain during World War II, was known for his inspirational speeches during a time of great turmoil. Perhaps his most famous speech, delivered on June 4, 1940, was titled "We Shall Fight on the Beaches". This speech, aimed at a French audience, declared that Britain's determination and courage in the face of Nazi aggression would not falter. In this speech, Churchill's words were both firm and inspiring. With his words, Churchill helped to rally the British nation and changed the course of the war.

When considering the impact of Winston Churchill's "We Shall Fight on the Beaches" speech, one must look at the implications of his words on the British people. His famous words encouraged the British population to look forward, no matter how dire the situation might seem. The phrase was a call to arms, not only to the military forces of Britain but to the civilians at home as well. Even in an age of sophisticated weaponry, Churchill understood the power of the human spirit in winning battles and ultimately a war.

By mentioning the beaches in his speech, Churchill was also emphasizing one of Britain's core defenses. As the speech was given following the surrender of France to the Nazi regime, the British people were now facing the prospect of a direct invasion. Churchill's speech sought to inspire a unified defense against this imminent threat. He emphasized the British nation's determination in the face of adversity, even in what appeared to be a hopeless situation.

The phrase "We Shall Fight on the Beaches" is so well known today due to the legacy of its effectiveness. Churchill inspired the British people with his speech and it is widely accepted that the words of this speech played a significant role in the efforts of Britain to resist Nazi aggression during World War II. Not only did the speech help to bolster public morale, but it also provided an invaluable reminder to the wartime leaders of Britain of what Britain was fighting for and why.

The "We Shall Fight on the Beaches" speech given by Winston Churchill had a great impact on the British people and their efforts in World War II. His rousing words encouraged many during a time of despair and reminded people of what was at stake and why it was important to continue the fight.

CHAPTER TEN

John F. Kennedy

John F. Kennedy - "Ask Not What Your Country Can Do for You" speech, delivered during his inaugural address in 1961.

John F. Kennedy's famous phrase "Ask not what your country can do for you — ask what you can do for your country" has served as an inspirational call-to-action for generations of Americans. Focusing on full participation and responsible citizenship, the famous phrase epitomizes the spirit of Kennedy's celebrated presidency.

When Kennedy delivered the speech to a large crowd of citizens gathered in the Capital in 1961, he spoke of a unified, committed nation that would work together to solve any challenges they faced. At the time, many Americans were facing the challenges of the Cold War and Kennedy used the opportunity to call for national service as a response. He argued that citizens should not demand what the government could do for them, but rather, look beyond national boundaries and strive to do their duty to the world.

Kennedy's "Ask not" phrase was the cornerstone of his

presidency and has become an iconic part of American culture. In the speech, he defined citizenship as an ongoing responsibility to help forge a better world and nation. Kennedy's words furthermore recognized America's international standing and its duty as global leader.

Rather than promote selfishness and complacency, the speech focused on selflessness and activism. The values of hard work and engagement were promoted in order to benefit society more broadly. At the same time, he challenged his audience to ask the relevant questions and to think beyond their own personal interests.

Many of Kennedy's initiatives and programs during his short lived presidency were shaped by the theme of his "Ask not" phrase. From boosting participation in the Peace Corps to creating initiatives that fostered racial equality, Kennedy consistently pushed citizens to be active members of their country and to consider the world outside of their own needs and desires.

John F. Kennedy's "Ask not" speech highlighted his commitment to citizens and the country. By using the metaphor of asking what an individual could do for his or her nation, Kennedy initiated a call-to-action which demanded full participation and global involvement. The phrase has come to symbolize the bold, unselfish spirit of Kennedy's presidency and serves as a defining statement of the power of citizens to make a positive impact on society.

CHAPTER ELEVEN

Mahalia Jackson

Mahalia Jackson - "I've Been 'Buked and I've Been Scorned" speech, delivered at the March on Washington in 1963.

Mahalia Jackson was one of the most influential gospel singers of all time. She is best known for her song "I've Been Buked, and I've Been Scorned." This song was written to inspire and give hope to those in the black community who had been oppressed and discriminated against.

The song's lyrics tell a story of suffering and resilience. Jackson sings, "I've been buked, and I've been scorned, a long time / I've been thrown 'way, but I'm still here / I've been deserted, and I've been left to mourn / But I still haven't forsaken my faith." These lyrics suggest that, despite being oppressed, she still believes and trusts in God, refusing to give up hope.

Although it was written about her personal experience, "I've Been Buked" became something of an anthem for the Civil Rights Movement. This song was particularly popular at the 1963 March on Washington, where it was performed by Mahalia Jackson. The song resonated with the struggles of many African Americans and symbolized the resilience and strength of the movement.

The lasting impact of "I've Been Buked" lies in the powerful message it conveys. Jackson used her music to speak out against oppression and inspire a sense of hope and solidarity. Through this song, she asserted the importance of standing together and not giving in to despair. This powerful refrain is still relevant today, as many people in society continue to fight for social justice.

The music of Mahalia Jackson will continue to have a lasting influence on future generations. Her song "I've Been Buked" stands as a reminder of the strength and courage of the oppressed, and a reminder that no matter how much suffering one might endure, there is still hope and love in the world. Through her resilient spirit and her powerful music, Mahalia Jackson left us a legacy of hope and resilience.

CHAPTER TWELVE

Cesar Chavez

Cesar Chavez - "Farm Workers and the American Dream" speech, delivered at the Commonwealth Club of California in 1984.

Cesar Chavez was a renowned leader, activist and human rights defender. He is best known for his fight for and on behalf of farm workers, who wanted to improve their living and working conditions, and to raise the bar on their salaries. On March 31, 1968, he gave a memorable speech that has had a lasting impact on the fight for improving conditions for farm workers, and helped reignite the national focus on civil rights.

In his speech, Chavez recounts his childhood memories of farm workers and how he, his family and friends had once toiled in the fields, picking grapes, lettuce and other crops. He eloquently points out that the farms on which he worked, and visits, had belonged to Mexicans and other Latinos who, in his words "poured their sweat into land and left no remnant of their toil." It was this experience that drove him to become a social justice advocate, fighting for economic justice for undeserved communities.

What followed in his speech is an impassioned plea for action, one that expressed the farmworkers' plight and reminded people that in the United States, democracy should mean something. Chavez speaks powerfully of the theft of land and property that the farm workers experience, and of the loss of free speech, free assembly, and freedom of speech. He insisted everyone had a right to a better wage and urged everyone to seek out solutions that would eventually help create a better justice system. He disagreed with the then-current system of wages, stating they were too low, meaning that "our people are being exploited and denied the rights that others enjoy." Chavez asked for people to recognise the plight of farm workers and unite to "emancipate" them from their oppression.

He used the speech to highlight the importance of working together, of petitions, and of "peaceful non-cooperation" as powerful tools to continue in the fight for justice. Chavez acknowledged the difficulties of the task, saying "it will take courage and dedication," but he was clear that it was up to "all of us" to continue the struggle. He was emphatic that such rights are enshrined not just in the US Constitution, but in the value of a democracy.

In summarising this stirring speech, Chavez ends with a powerful message. He talks of how impossible it is for the "all-American dream of justice, freedom and equality" to be achieved without the involvement of all people. He stressed how the farmworkers needed to be respected in order for the ideal of the American Dream to become a reality.

The speech from Cesar Chavez marked the beginning of a movement that fought for the rights of the farmworkers, and it reinforced his proactive reputation as a leader and public speaker. It resonated far and wide, and his words continue to inspire people around the world.

CHAPTER THIRTEEN

George Washington

George Washington - "Farewell Address" speech, delivered in 1796.

Since his election to the office of President of the United States in 1789, George Washington had established a precedent of presidential behaviour that future presidents would strive to follow. On September 17th, 1796, Washington delivered his Farewell Address speech and addressed the many reasons why his advice would be important for the future of the United States. In this historically significant address, Washington highlighted the integral role of morality and virtue in a nation's wellbeing, stressing the need for citizens to rely on religion and morality to foster good national morals. He also talked about the importance of having a united nation, and encouraged a sense of bipartisanship and unity amongst the citizens and politicians in Washington D.C.

At the speech's start, Washington opens by expressing his gratitude for the opportunity to serve his fellow citizens as the country's first President. He briefly touches on the developments made during his two terms and how he hopes they will last "for ages to come". Washington then shifts his focus to the moral state of the nation and explains how an absence of virtue and morality can "tend to dissolution of the Union". He stresses the need for citizens to rely on religion and morality to form a strong foundation to the country. Without strong foundations, Washington believes the nation will be doomed to failure and fragmentation.

Through his address, Washington also muses about the power of opinion and its attachment to party politics. On the one hand, he states that the spirit of party and faction can be "useful", as it can provide a healthy outlet of political expression. However, he argues against blind partisanship, promoting the idea that "all obstructions to the execution of the laws" need to be avoided. Washington argues strenuously for the need to develop national unity and warns against providing too much attention to individual views of party. He then moves on to discuss institutional issues, stressing the need for strong institutions that will provide stability and order to the nation.

Throughout his speech, Washington also encourages friendly relations with other countries. He implores the nation to avoid long-term entanglements, and instead urges the nation to work on developing normal, cooperative relationships. Furthermore, Washington stresses the importance of remaining "free from foreign influence and attachments". He explains that this will be crucial for maintaining national security and protecting the nation's interests.

In the address's conclusion, Washington expresses the need for citizens to be vigilant in protecting the nation's laws and institutions and to learn to be patient and tolerant of each other. Ultimately, Washington's address serves as a reminder for us all that true progress can only be achieved when citizens adopt strong morals, remain keen participants in politics, and strive for national unity.

Swami Vivekananda

Swami Vivekananda - "Sisters and Brothers of America" speech, delivered at the Parliament of the World's Religions in Chicago in 1893.

Swami Vivekananda's historic 'Sisters and Brothers of America' speech at the 1893 World's Parliament of Religions in Chicago was cited as the beginning of modern Hinduism in North America. Widely regarded as a benchmark for Hindu-Western intellectual exchange, it involved religious and spiritual discussion, combining ideas of East and West, and articulation of religious reform within both civilizations.

His speech had three main objectives. First, he highlighted the essential identity between all religions, citing them as means to reach the union between the individual soul and the omnipresent, eternal Paramatman. He identified the teachings of Shri Ramakrishna and praised the Vedic principles of 'freedom of soul.' Secondly, he explained Hinduism's history, as well as its stigma as primitive and disdainful. He also discussed India's trials with foreign invasion and cultural divide between the north and south, along with the discrimination and poverty they created. He went on to draw an analogy between the monastic order of the yogis and the Protestant faith in the west. Lastly, Swami Vivekananda discussed what knowledge the west could offer to India, like science and the rationalism of the west, to promote better education and health. He also spoke about the west's ability to provide for the basic needs of India's poor, such as food and shelter.

Swami Vivekananda's speech was not only a religious discourse, but also an expression of his defiance against the social and political wrongs of the British Raj. Even then, he spoke of spiritual growth as the true goal for both East and West. He encouraged coexistence and respect, unifying ideas of Eastern and Western philosophies. He called for unity in order to solve the obstacles faced by both cultures and praised American egalitarianism and its major role in religious reform.

Finally, Vivekananda concluded his speech with a statement to "hold all the world as one family", encouraging men and women of all religions to join him in pursuit of knowledge and spiritual growth. His speech seduced many within the Parliament and is still referenced today as a founding argument for intercontinental dialogue between the East and West.

Swami Vivekananda's 'Sisters and Brothers of America' speech effectively captured the religions and perspectives of both Eastern and Western people. His idealistic perspective for a planetary shift towards coexistence, compassion and peace serve as a model for harmonious cultures and the betterment of all humanity.

CHAPTER FIFTEEN

Apj Abdul Kalam

Apj Abdul Kalam - "Vision of India 2020" speech, delivered as the President of India in 2011.

On March 17, 2020, former President, Professor Avul Pakir Jainulabdeen Abdul Kalam, delivered one of his most famous speeches – 'India 2020: Vision of My Dream' in the New Delhi YMCA. Through this speech, he aimed to inspire the nation to strive for progress and shared a detailed vision of India that he wanted to see by the year 2020.

Abdul Kalam's speech started off with him focussing on the need to make India an 'educated and developed country', by embracing innovative technologies, reducing poverty, and reinforcing its strong democratic foundation. He emphasized the need to utilise the potential of human resources across the nation and utilize them to their full capacity. Moreover, he elaborated on the importance of education, and likened it to be the 'most powerful weapon' that could be used to assure the nation's growth and development.

Abdul Kalam also addressed the issue of poverty and suggested avenues of how to tackle it. He proposed the need to revolutionize the agricultural industry and make it more productive so that people from the rural parts of the country are better equipped with resources. Furthermore, he advocated that the government should work towards making the agricultural industry more financially viable, so that it can play an even bigger role in ensuring economic prosperity.

He then talked about the need to take care of the environment and pointed out the ill-effects of excessive industrialisation and pollution. He spoke about how it was important to invest in renewable energy sources and curb the carbon dioxide emission by holding industries accountable for their actions.

Abdul Kalam digressed to talk about his vision of India as a strong military power, equipped with the latest technological developments. He highlighted India's need to build a strong nuclear system while simultaneously emphasizing the need to develop and prioritize non-conventional modes of warfare.

He concluded his speech by emphasizing the need for a strong foundation of unity and justice that would help India become an industrialized modern nation. He also motivated the country to become an influential member of the international community and rally around minorities, the deprived and the poverty-stricken.

Abdul Kalam's speech had a vision of transforming the nation into a developed one by the end of 2020. It encouraged the people to focus on developing education, solving the issues of poverty, environment and pollution, and becoming a force to reckon with in the international community. It reiterated the power of unity and justice that could enable the nation to be resilient and become a great leader of the world. Abdul Kalam's legacy remains an inspiration to generations of Indians even in the present times.

Other Books Of The Author

1. The Moments When I Met God
2. Kashiyile Theertha Pathangal
3. GURU GYAN VANI
4. Abhiprerak Gita
5. ASSI SE JAIN GHAT TAK
6. Hopelessness of Arjuna
7. The Soul and It's True Nature
8. Sense of Action (Karma)
9. Action through Wisdom
10. Action through Wisdom
11. THEORY AND PRACTICAL OF EVERY ACTION
12. LOGICAL UNDERSTANDING OF THE SUPREME
13. THE IMPERISHABLE SUPREME
14. Yatra Nishadraj se Hanuman Ghat Tak
15. Yatra Karnatak Ghat se Raja Ghat Tak
16. Yatra Pandey Ghat se Prayagraj Ghat Tak
17. Yatra Ranjendra Prasad Ghat se Dattatreya Ghat Tak
18. YaatraSindhiya Ghat se Gwaliar Ghat Tak
19. Yatra Mangala Gauri Ghat se Hanuman Gadhi Ghat Tak
20. Yatra Gaay Ghat Se Nishad Ghat Tak
21. MAA GANGA, GHATEN EVM UTSAV
22. Ganga Arti Dev Deepavali evam Any Utsav
23. Potentials of Digitalized India
24. VEDIC CONSCIOUSNESS
25. A Brief Introduction to Vedic Science
26. Kashi ke Barah Jyotirling
27. IMPACT OF MOTIVATION
28. Let's have a Milky Way Journey
29. Color Therapy in a Nutshell

59. "The Holistic Cow: A Look at the Physical, Spiritual, and Cultural Importance of Cows in India"
60. Five Elements

Contact

DR. JAGADEESH PILLAI

PhD in Vedic Science

Four Times Guinness World Record Holder

Winner of Mahatma Gandhi Vishwa Shanti Puraskar and Global Peace Ambassador

Gemology, Astro & Vastu Consultant - Spiritual Counselor

Consultant for designing World Record Ideas

Efficient Tarot Card Reader

9839093003

myrichindia@gmail.com

drjagadeeshpillai@facebook

drjagadeeshpillai@instagram

jagadeeshpillai@youtube

www. JAGADEESHPILLAI.com

|| LOKAHA SAMASTHAHA SUKHINO BHAVANTU ||

• 45 •